Coronado
Searches for
Cities of Gold

by Josie Black

Contents

Life in New Spain

Spain had many **colonies** across the ocean in the 1500s. One colony was a place called New Spain, the area known as Mexico today. The king of Spain sent a man named Antonio de Mendoza to rule for him in the colony. In 1535 Mendoza set sail for New Spain. He brought a helper with him—Francisco Vásquez (VAS kes) de Coronado.

In Mexico City Coronado served in the government. Then Mendoza made him **governor** of an area called New Galicia. Life was good for Coronado, but change was coming.

Coronado (on horse) was a governor of part of New Spain.

Stories of Cities of Gold

Old Spanish stories told of seven cities filled with riches. Some people thought the cities might be in the area north of New Spain.

In 1536 an explorer named Cabeza (ka BAY sah) de Vaca said he had seen cities of gold. De Vaca had come to New Spain with a slave named Esteban (eh STAY bawn) and two other men. They had walked more than 1,000 miles. The four were the last members of an **expedition** that had gone to North America in 1528. Mendoza was very interested in their stories of golden cities.

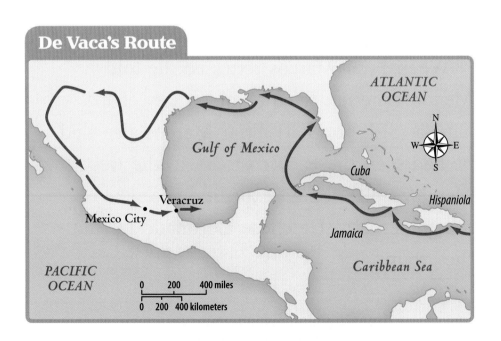

De Vaca's Route

Mendoza sent Friar Marcos de Niza to lead the scouting party.

Mendoza wanted to know if these stories were true. He asked Friar Marcos de Niza (NEE sah) to lead a group to the north. Esteban, the slave, went as a guide because he knew the way.

When Friar Marcos returned, he told Mendoza he had seen a golden city called Cíbola (SEE boh lah). Friar Marcos also said he had seen the Pacific Ocean to the west. Mendoza planned an expedition to take over the golden city. He chose Coronado to lead the group.

The Search for Gold Begins

Coronado's expedition began in February of 1540 with hundreds of soldiers and slaves. The group brought cattle, sheep, and horses. More supplies went on ships to meet them later.

A smaller group, including Coronado and Friar Marcos, went ahead of the expedition. It was a long, hard journey. The group did not find **landmarks** where the friar said they would. By June their horses were dying from the heat. The group had little food, and they did not know how to find the ships.

Coronado's expedition left New Galicia in 1540.

Arriving at Hawikuh

When Coronado came to the place where Friar Marcos said Cíbola would be, he did not see a city of gold. He saw a simple **pueblo** of Zuñi (ZOON yee) Native Americans. The Zuñi called their town of sun-baked mud homes Hawikuh (ha WEE kuh).

By this time Coronado's men were very hungry, so they attacked Hawikuh to get food and supplies. The Spanish had better weapons, and they had horses. They forced the Native Americans out of Hawikuh.

Coronado's soldiers began to grow angry at Friar Marcos. He had not told the truth about Cíbola. There was no gold in the city. Friar Marcos feared that the soldiers might hurt him, so Coronado sent the friar back to New Spain.

Coronado did not give up. He decided to continue the expedition. He still hoped to find cities of gold.

His group remained in Hawikuh because there was plenty of food there. From Hawikuh Coronado sent out three groups to search for the golden cities.

The expedition found only a pueblo called Hawikuh.

Exploring from Hawikuh

Each of Coronado's groups set out in a different direction. The group led by Don García López de Cárdenas went to the northwest. They had heard stories about a large river to the west. Cárdenas did not find gold, but he hoped to find a river route for supply ships.

The group found the Colorado River deep in the beautiful Grand Canyon. Cárdenas thought the river looked too small for their ships, but his men were the first Europeans to see the Grand Canyon.

Cárdenas and his group saw the Grand Canyon.

Melchior (MEL kyor) Díaz's group tried to find a route to the Pacific Ocean. They hoped to meet the supply ships. Near what is now California, they found a message from the ships' commander. The letter said that the ships had been there but had already returned to New Spain.

The men in Díaz's group reached California. They had not found gold or the Pacific Ocean, though. The group headed back to Hawikuh.

Díaz's men were the first Europeans in California.

Coronado sent Hernando de Alvarado's group to find other cities. Alvarado's guide for the trip was a Native American chief called Bigotes.

The group found Tiguex (tee GWESH) in what is now New Mexico. The city had no gold. There were many pueblos for shelter, though, and grass for the horses. Alvarado told Coronado about the area. Coronado decided that the expedition would stay at Tiguex through the winter.

Alvarado explored parts of the Great Plains and saw herds of buffalo.

The Tiguex War

While he waited for Coronado to arrive in Tiguex, Alvarado explored the area to the east. A Native American guide called "the Turk" helped the Spanish find buffalo herds there. The Turk also talked about a city of gold called Quivira (kee VEE rah).

While exploring this area, the Turk and Bigotes had a disagreement. Alvarado took the Turk's side, and he made Bigotes a prisoner. Back in Tiguex, Alvarado put Bigotes in chains.

These ruins at the Coronado State Monument are where Tiguex once stood.

The Native Americans in Tiguex did not like the fact that Bigotes was in chains. They began to distrust the Spanish. Things got worse when winter came and the Spanish began taking food, blankets, and clothing from the natives.

Then some of the natives stole horses from Coronado. He ordered his men to attack the people of Tiguex and to follow any of them who ran away. The Spanish killed hundreds of Native Americans in the Tiguex War.

No Gold in Quivira

In the spring of 1541, Coronado led his men east to claim the gold of Quivira. The Turk guided the group. It took them months to make the journey. When they arrived they found only a simple village of straw huts.

Coronado explored the land around Quivira, but there were no riches to be found. The Turk had lied to them, and Coronado had him killed. The Spanish went back to Tiguex for the winter.

A Native American guide called "the Turk" led Coronado's expedition to Quivira.

Coronado Fails

That winter Coronado finally realized that he would not find any cities of gold. He decided to go back to New Spain. Coronado would have to tell Mendoza that he had failed.

The group returned to Mexico City in 1542. Mendoza was angry that the expedition had failed. He put Coronado on trial. In 1554 Mendoza even took away Coronado's job as governor of New Galicia. Coronado died that year in Mexico City.

Coronado was buried at this church in Mexico City.

A Look Back at the Journey

Francisco Vásquez de Coronado had hoped to find the seven cities of gold. When he learned that there was no gold to be found, his expedition was considered a **failure**. However, the expedition was very successful in other ways.

Coronado's men were the first Europeans to see the **Great Plains**, the Grand Canyon, and the Colorado River. They spent time at Native American pueblos. Coronado failed to find gold. Yet he succeeded at gaining a great deal of information about the people and land of the Southwest.

Coronado actually achieved a great deal on his expedition.

Glossary

colonies places that are ruled by a
country that is far away

expedition a journey made by a group
of people for a particular purpose

failure lack of success

governor the ruler of part of a country
or region

Great Plains flat land with tall grasses
in the middle of the United States

landmarks parts of land that mark a
location, such as large rocks or rivers

pueblo a Native American dwelling
made of dried mud